D1403124

BAROQUE AND ROMANTIC
STAGE DESIGN

JÁNOS SCHOLZ is a well-known 'cello virtuoso in addition to being a discriminating art collector and connoisseur. He owns one of the foremost American private collections of early Italian drawings and has lectured at both Columbia and New York Universities on Italian drawings and connoisseurship in addition to writing many articles and book reviews in this field. Mr. Scholz is also the editor of *Theatrical Designs from the Baroque Through Neoclassicism* (1940).

A. HYATT MAYOR has for many years been the Curator of Prints at the Metropolitan Museum of Art, New York. He is a graduate of Princeton University and was a Rhodes Scholar at Oxford. Mr. Mayor taught the history of art at Vassar College and was also the co-editor of *Hound and Horn* before joining the staff of the Metropolitan Museum in 1932. He is the author of *The Bibiena Family* (1945) and *Giovanni Battista Piranesi* (1952), plus many articles in art magazines.

BAROQUE AND ROMANTIC STAGE DESIGN was first published in 1950.

Note: The stage designs reproduced on the covers of this book are the work of the following artists.

Front cover, top: *Design for a City Square* by Giuseppe Bibiena.

Front cover, bottom: *Design for a Courtyard* by Giovanni Battista Piranesi.

Back cover, top: *Design for a Courtyard* by Giuseppe Bibiena.

BAROQUE AND ROMANTIC
STAGE DESIGN

Edited by

János Scholz 1368

Introduction by

A. Hyatt Mayor

A Dutton  *Paperback*

NEW YORK
E. P. DUTTON & CO., INC.
1962

This paperback edition of
"BAROQUE AND ROMANTIC
STAGE DESIGN"
Published 1962 by E. P. Dutton & Co., Inc.
All rights reserved. Printed in the U.S.A.

Copyright, 1949, by H. Bittner & Company, New York, N.Y.
Reprinted by special arrangement with the
Henry Regnery Company, Chicago, Illinois

Published simultaneously in Canada by Clarke,
Irwin and Company Limited, Toronto and Vancouver.

general effect is red and brown. It is curious that a variety of bright water-colours, like those in mediaeval illuminations and Dürer's early travel sketches, could not be bought easily until London dealers began to stock them a little before 1800. Paul Sandby (1725-1809) is the first water-colourist who started by tinting ink drawings and ended with an almost modern range of pigments. When he died, the stage was also beginning to show landscapes in the full colours of noon and sundown.

But within a colour range as limited as the orchestral colour of the concerto grosso, the baroque theatre achieved marvels still unsurpassed. One of the few places where we today can form some picture of the poetic majesty of the old theatre is the banqueting hall at Greenwich College on the Thames. As one turns the stairs, the great room comes into view when the eye is level with the floor. Every foot of the largely windowed hall is painted in leaf brown shadowed with the bloom of purple grapes and accented in October gold. Right and left, the flanking processions of window embrasures are decorated symmetrically, like the flats in the baroque stage. At the far end a flight of steps and a tall arch frame a backdrop painted with drapery billowing among columns, with noble allegories dominating from clouds, and royalty indicating the horizons of their power. Few rooms in the world achieve splendor with such plain means. Where marble and bronze would have crushed with durability, this film of scaling paint is human—here today and gone tomorrow, like us. The even frailer canvases of the old theatre, quivering in the glimmer of candles, must have touched the heart with an exquisite magic of evanescence. It is no wonder that after the fall of the baroque style, baroque architectural effects continued to hold the stage intermittently through Romanticism and Realism as the ideal to which the theatre has always returned when it would cast a spell of sumptuousness.

A. HYATT MAYOR

CATALOGUE

IN 1940 Herbert Bittner published a book on stage design, for which George Freedley wrote an introduction and this writer selected the pictures. This book, called *Theatrical Designs from the Baroque Through Neoclassicism*, was issued in a limited edition of one hundred and twenty-five copies, and has long been out of print. The present more comprehensive publication, first issued in 1950, covers a longer stretch of time and includes many drawings that have never been reproduced before. The illustrations appear in more or less chronological order to show the development of stage decoration during its age of glory.

Most of the drawings included in this book come from two main sources: the collection of Michael Mayr (1796-1870), stage designer to the Princes Eszterházy in Eisenstadt, Austria, and the collection of Giovanni Piancastelli (1844-1926), in Rome.

The collection formed by Michael Mayr has an interesting history. This Austrian-born artist was quite a popular stage designer during the first decades of the nineteenth century in Vienna. His early years were spent studying at the Imperial Academy of Fine Arts and in earning his keep painting sets for suburban theatres. Mayr also seems to have had quite an inventive mind, which made him famous and sought after in theatrical circles. Among the friends who helped him gain fame and fortune were such men as Raimund, Lanner, and Strauss. We can assume that he started to acquire large groups of drawings by Viennese designers during these years of success and affluence.

Unfortunately, however, his very inventiveness brought hard times to Mayr. An attempt to popularize a kind of mechanical-optical theatre or peepshow backfired and ended in disaster; he was forced to leave Vienna. Taking refuge in the delightful Hungarian border town called Eisenstadt, he began painting for his own pleasure, mainly views of the neighboring countryside, and later on also stage sets and decorations for the Eszterházy princes who still lived, surrounded by a certain aura of splendor, in their magnificent castle. Soon he amassed another sizable fortune and was able to live out the last twenty-five years of his life in grace and comfort until his death in 1870.

As a stage designer, Michael Mayr is a solid mixture of all that the great Viennese theatre tradition around 1800 could offer. Undoubtedly, he is more of a painter then a meticulous follower of the earlier fanatics of stage perspective. His study collection included drawings and prints by the Bibiena family, works by the great Venetians, and originals by the Piedmontese theatre architects. All these left a strong imprint upon his style, lending substantial solidity to his pleasing compositions. Who his teachers were among the then-famous Viennese stage designers is not firmly established. But from the amount of material he owned by Norbert Bittner and Antonio de Pian, both his seniors by hardly a generation, we can assume that he worked with them.

Josef Platzer, however, was the real genius among the Viennese stage architects of the late eighteenth century; he combined the talent of an easel painter with the qualifications necessary for a virtuoso decorator. His profound knowledge of scenic design was anchored in the best Bibiena and Piranesi tradition and saturated with his admiration for and adherence to the rules laid down by his great predecessors. Next to the Academy of Fine Arts in Vienna, Michael Mayr owned the largest portion of this designer's *oeuvre*. The many hundreds of working sketches and finished projects found in the Eisenstadt portfolios were probably acquired by Mayr through Norbert Bittner, who was the engraver and publisher of Platzer's inventions. That the younger artist studied these is obvious; that he subconsciously, or even consciously at times, used some of the material was inevitable.

Mayr's really important accomplishment, though, was the heritage he left for posterity by amassing and conserving this extraordinarily rich collection of theatre material which he searched out with the sagacity and passion of a real explorer. He must have purchased almost every scrap of paper that the great Viennese designers of the Napoleonic period left in their studios after their deaths. The Mayr Collection shows the history of the theatre in a continuous line from the Bibienas down to his own time.

Among the famous Italian artists working in the Imperial capital, Lorenzo Sacchetti was very well represented in Eisenstadt. This Venetian became one of the most celebrated artists in the Hapsburg empire; he traveled extensively, mostly between Vienna and Prague, where he published a book on stage design in 1830. He was still alive in 1834, at which time he designed a group of classical inventions in the Piranesi manner, and contained in a small album bearing the date above and the place where he drew them, Pilsen in Bohemia (Museum of Fine Arts, Budapest).

Sacchetti must also have owned the spectacular sketch-book by his master, Domenico Fossati, which came to light in the Mayr Collection. Recent research, and also a small album in the Princeton University Art Museum bearing an inscription by Sacchetti, in which he claims to be a pupil of Fossati, has proved correct my earlier assumption of this master-pupil relationship, arrived at through comparison and study of style and execution. Another famous Venetian, Bernardo Belotto, who passed through Vienna on his way from Dresden to Warsaw, figured in the Mayr Collection with a small sketch-book containing close to fifty pages, in addition to quite a few loose drawings; this lot must be considered as the most important in size and significance after the well-known group in the National Museum in Warsaw.

Antonio de Pian, another Venetian who worked for many years in Vienna and almost became an indigenous Austrian, also left a good-sized *oeuvre* which was engraved by Norbert Bittner and published in 1818. The number of originals by this designer found in Mayr's Eisenstadt collection leads to the almost obvious assumption that the younger artist knew De Pian and may have even worked with him. There is no doubt that Mayr's *oeuvre* in many ways shows affinities which indicate a master-pupil relationship rather than just an admiration *par distance* or adaptation bordering closely on copying.

There are no indications from which source the considerable number of drawings by members of the great Piedmontese family of stage architects, the Galliari, came into the portfolios of the Mayr Collection. Since the publication of the first Bittner volumes and also the first edition of the present book a good deal of information has been unearthed by the eminent Italian Galliari-scholar, Mercedes Viale-Ferrero. According to her findings, two of the drawings in the present volume (nos. 50 and 51), traditionally given to Bernardino Galliari, should be assigned to his younger brother Fabrizio, who was the most active stage designer among the members of this famous clan.

In addition to the aforementioned group of Platzer drawings and those of the Italians, Michael Mayr owned works by almost every native Austrian designer of his time. There seemed to be a sort of friendly exchange of works among these artists, as several inscriptions of quite whimsical nature on a few sheets of the collection clearly indicate. He kept not only the fine things generously given to him, but also every scrap or note. Mayr's house was a treasure trove for anyone interested in almost any aspect of the theatre: playbills, letters, dedicated portraits, mementos, manuscripts, libretti, musical autographs, and a most interesting series of his own biographical notes which shed light on many phases of the political, artistic, and everyday life of Austro-Hungary during the first half of the nineteenth century.

Mayr's Eisenstadt collection was discovered intact, about 1930, in the possession of a descendant, Miss Marianne Fájt, who kept it religiously until circumstances forced her to sell part of it. The owner of a local private museum, Sándor Wolf, bought this large first group, but after he had to leave Eisenstadt for political reasons, most of his material was transferred to the county museum. Later on, some of these drawings were returned to the Wolf family and subsequently sold. A large portion was acquired from Miss Fájt by this writer in 1939 and brought to New York; all the drawings in this book, indicated in the catalogue as originally coming from the Mayr-Fájt Collection, were selected from this latter group. Some of the drawings remaining with Miss Fájt found their way into the National Library in Vienna, and those remaining were divided among several friends after the owner's death about 1955. Another large lot from this last source turned up recently in Austria and is at present in the New York art market.

The collection of drawings once belonging to Giovanni Piancastelli is also of great interest, especially for us Americans. This Emilian painter and collector, who was for some time the curator of the Borghese pictures in Rome, acquired almost everything he could lay his hands on in Rome and Naples during the latter part of the nineteenth century and thus formed a vast assemblage of drawings of all periods, descriptions, and quality. Just how large this collection was we do not know, but it must have numbered at least fifteen thousand items. In 1901 the Cooper-Hewitts of New York purchased a large group of drawings from Piancastelli in Rome. Two years later, in 1903, there was a sale in Rome of part of Piancastelli's collection. The Brandegee family of Boston bought generously at this sale, and in 1904 they acquired privately still more drawings from the same collection. The drawings acquired by the Hewitt family went to the Cooper Union Museum for the Arts of Decoration in New York, while the Brandegee lot remained undisturbed for many years in their mansion in Brookline, Massachusetts. In 1938 the Cooper Union Museum bought about eleven thousand drawings from the Brandegees, among them over four hundred drawings for stage sets by the great Italian masters, and whole groups of works by Valadier, Giani, Bison, and others. Piancastelli at one time had a most remarkable lot of drawings by various members of the Bibiena family, most of which are now in the Poliaghi Collection in Varese. But in 1944 another large lot was found in the Brandegee house, among which were about fifty drawings by the Bibienas and their immediate followers. This lot was acquired by the present writer and is partly reproduced here for the first time. From this same source also comes the fine stage set by Giovanni Battista Piranesi (no. 69), now belonging to Mr. Henry Regnery of Hinsdale, Illinois.

Since the publication of the first edition of this volume in 1950, all drawings listed in the catalogue as belonging to this writer, except nos. 13, 68, and 70, have passed into the collection of the distinguished American stage designer, Donald Oenslager of New York. The publishers and the editor are grateful to Mr. Oenslager for permitting the reproduction of his fine drawings here.

The editor is indebted to the following collectors and institutions for kindly lending their material to help to make this publication a success: Walter C. Baker, New York; Hans M. Calmann, London; the late A. M. Friend, Jr., Princeton, New Jersey; Walter Hugelshofer, Zurich; The Cooper Union Museum for the Arts of Decoration, New York; the Metropolitan Museum of Art, New York, and the New York Public Library.

The editor is also sincerely thankful for the most valuable help given to him so generously by his friend A. Hyatt Mayor and to Rudolf Berliner; but above all to the memory of the late Herbert Bittner, without whose knowledge and initiative as a publisher this book never would have been made.

New York City   JÁNOS SCHOLZ
May, 1962

È, VINCENZO DAL
Died 1762.

FOUNTAIN, COURTYARD AND STAIRS.
Pen and wash.

572-705 mm.

Coll.: Janos Scholz, New York.

(on pages 14 and 15)

PERUZZI, BALDASSARE
1481–1536.

Architect and painter, worked in Siena
and Rome.

STREET SCENE; LEFT HALF OF A STAGE
SET.

Pen, bistre.

Turin, Biblioteca del Palazzo Reale.

PUBLIC SQUARE, WITH RENAISSANCE
BUILDINGS AND SOME ROMAN RUINS.

Pen, bistre wash.

Florence, Uffizi.

SERLIO, SEBASTIANO
1475–1554.

Architect and painter, pupil of Baldassare Peruzzi, worked in Rome, Venice, Is-
tria, Dalmatia, died in Fontainebleau.

SCENA COMICA.

Woodcut.

From: Il Secondo Libro di Perspettiva,
Paris, 1545.

SCAMOZZI, VINCENZO
1552–1616.

Architect, born in Vicenza, worked in Vicenza, Venice, Rome, Florence, Bologna,
died in Venice.

4 DRAWING FOR A STREET SCENE.

Pen, bistre.

Florence, Uffizi.

5 DRAWING FOR A STREET SCENE WITH A
CLASSICAL CIRCULAR TEMPLE.

Pen, bistre.

This and the previous drawing are sets
designed for the permanent stage of the
Teatro Olimpico in Vicenza.

Florence, Uffizi.

PERUZZI, SALLUSTIO
Died 1573.

Architect, son of Baldassare Peruzzi.

6 TWO STAGE SETS ON ONE PAGE; ON THE
TOP: STREET SCENE WITH A CIRCULAR
TEMPLE IN THE BACK; ON THE BOTTOM:
ANOTHER VERSION OF THE SAME SCENE,
WITH ONLY ONE SIDE FINISHED. BUILD-
INGS WITH COLONNADES, STAIRS LEADING
UP TO THE STAGE, WITH A CIRCULAR
PLATFORM ON THE PROSCENIUM.

Pen, bistre wash.

215-140 mm.

There are similar drawings by Sallustio
Peruzzi in the Uffizi.

Colls.: Piancastelli, Brandegee.

Janos Scholz, New York.

PARIGI, GIULIO
Died 1635.

Architect and engraver, pupil of B. Buontalenti. Worked mostly in Florence.

7 "AVVISO DI MERCURIO A BERECINTA DEA
DELLA TERRA ET ALLE NINFE DE CAMPI."
Set for *Sbarco di Venere.*
1628.
Engraving.

8 "INTERMEDIO QUINTO DI VULCANO."
1608.
Engraving by Remigio Cantagallina after Parigi.
This and the above stage set were made for the Medici-Festivals in Florence.

BUONTALENTI, BERNARDO
1536–1608.
Architect, painter, worked in Florence, Pisa, Siena and Livorno.

9 STREET SCENE.
1589.
Engraving by Orazio Scarabelli after Buontalenti.
For the marriage festivities of Christina of Lorraine and Ferdinando Medici III in Florence.

10 NAVAL BATTLE IN THE COURTYARD OF THE PALAZZO PITTI.
Engraving by Orazio Scarabelli after Buontalenti.
Probably for the same festivities as the above engraving.

TORELLI, GIACOMO
1604–1678.
Stage designer, born in Fano, worked in Venice, Paris and Fano.

11 HARBOR SCENE.
For: *Il Bellerofonte, Drama Musicale del*

Sig. Vincenzo Nolfi da F(ano) Rappresentato nel Teatro Novissimo in Venetia.
1642.
Engraving.

SANTURINI, FRANCESCO
1627–1682.
Stage designer, born in Venice, worked and died in Munich.

12 SCENE XI FOR "FEDRA INCORONATA" BY
PIETRO PAOLO BISSARI.
Munich, 1662.
Engraving.
Published by J. Jekel, Munich.

BELLA, STEFANO DELLA
1610–1664.
Painter and engraver, worked chiefly in Florence; he was employed by the Medici in connection with their various festivals.

13 COUNCIL OF THE KNIGHTS OF MALTA.
Pen, bistre over black chalk, gray wash.
Upper corners slanted.
268-404 mm.
The drawing was probably made during the artist's stay in Rome; it is an interesting example of a spectacular meeting conceived almost as a theatrical set with the figures on both sides of the drawing acting as side wings and lending depth to the whole picture.
Colls.: Unidentified Italian eighteenth century mark, Goldstein.
Janos Scholz, New York.

GUERCINO, GIOVANNI FRANCESCO BARBIERI

1591–1666.

Painter, born in Cento, near Bologna.

A THEATRE PERFORMANCE, PROBABLY IN CENTO.

Pen, bistre wash.

360-465 mm.

Coll.: Beurdeley.

London, British Museum.

BURNACINI, LODOVICO OTTAVIO

1636–1707.

Stage designer, born in Vienna where he worked most of his life.

THE TEMPLE OF VESTA.

Stage set for the opera *Il Fuoco Eterno,* text by Minato, music by Draghi and Schmelzer.

Engraving by M. Kuessel after Burnacini.

For the festivals on the occasion of the birth of Archduchess Anna Maria, daughter of Leopold I in Vienna, 1674.

SCIPIO'S PALACE.

Engraving by M. Kuessel after Burnacini.

For the same opera.

POZZO, ANDREA

1642–1709.

Painter, architect and writer, worked in Rome, Northern Italy and Vienna.

DRAWING FOR A "THEATRUM SACRUM"; LEFT PORTION.

Pen, bistre, brown and gray washes.

412-168 mm.

Although there are quite considerable differences between this drawing and the following engraving, the missing sculptures, the changed top structure, all of which give the drawing a more classical appearance, I would consider this drawing as by Pozzo and for the engraving; the pen work and the use of various washes are identical with some of the artist's authenticated drawings.

Colls.: Mayr, Fajt.

Janos Scholz, New York.

18 "THEATRUM SACRUM."

Engraving from: *Perspectiva Pictorum et Architectorum,* Rome, 1693.

MANTUAN ARTIST, about 1650

19 COURTYARD OF A PALACE, WITH PROSCENIUM.

Arms of the Duchy of Mantua on the top of the main arch.

Pen, bistre wash over black chalk.

331-455 mm.

This interesting drawing was identified and published by Dr. R. Berliner in the *Chronicle of the Museum for the Arts of Decoration of the Cooper Union,* vol. I, no. 8.

Colls.: Piancastelli, Brandegee.

Cooper Union Museum, New York.

MIDDLE ITALY, about 1650

20 PALACE COURTYARD WITH ARCHWAY LEADING INTO A PARK.

Signed P. V. interlaced.

Pen, bistre wash.

350-520 mm.

Probably made by a close follower of Torelli.

Colls.: Piancastelli, Brandegee.

Cooper Union Museum, New York.

MIDDLE ITALY, late seventeenth century

21 STAIRCASE AND HALL WITH COLUMNS.

Left portion of a backdrop.

Pen, bistre.

294-188 mm.

This drawing was published by the editor in *Theatrical Designs from the Baroque through Neoclassicism,* New York, 1940, vol. I, pl. 2, as by Ferdinando Galli Bibiena. After careful study I would like to modify my opinion and place the origin of this drawing somewhere between Bologna and Rome on account of its rather strong and very individual rhythm, its solidity of architecture not to be found in any of the Bibiena's work. I appreciate the firm and well-supported opinion of Hyatt Mayor, who helped me greatly to reconsider my former attribution and to place this fine example for the time being among the anonymous stage designers.

Colls.: Mayr, Fajt.

Janos Scholz, New York.

BIBIENA, FERDINANDO GALLI
1657–1743.

Stage designer, architect.

For the biographies of the Bibienas, see A. Hyatt Mayor: *The Bibiena Family,* New York, 1945.

22 INTERIOR OF A BEDROOM.

Right portion of a stage set.

Pen, bistre, brown and gray wash.

228-167 mm.

Published: A. H. Mayor: *The Bibiena Family,* pl. 7.

Colls.: Lamponi, Holford, Goldstein, Bloch.

A. M. Friend, Princeton, New Jersey.

23 LEFT PORTION OF A SET FOR A LARGE HALL WITH COLUMNS.

Pen, bistre, brown and gray washes.

201-133 mm.

Colls.: Piancastelli, Brandegee.

Herbert Bittner, New York.

24 RIGHT PORTION OF A SET FOR A HALL.

Pen, bistre wash.

408-283 mm.

On the back of this drawing is an inscription in the handwriting of Maria Ester Galli-Bibiena: *Originale di Ferdinando Galli, Bolognese 1701.*

Colls.: Piancastelli, Brandegee.

Henry Regnery, Hinsdale, Illinois.
See fig. 37.

25 PALACE COURTYARD.

Pen, bistre, greenish-gray wash.

215-270 mm.

Design for a plate in *Varie Opere di Prospettiva* by Ferdinando; this drawing was identified and published by A. Hyatt Mayor, *The Bibiena Family,* pl. 10.

Coll.: Cornelius Vanderbilt.

Metropolitan Museum of Art, New York.

26 COLONNADES WITH A FOUNTAIN, ARCHWAYS LEADING INTO A PALACE COURTYARD.

Pen, bistre, gray wash, blue water-colour.
233-298 mm.
Published: *Theatrical Designs*, vol. I, pl. 1.
Colls.: Mayr, Fajt.
Janos Scholz, New York.

BIBIENA, GIUSEPPE GALLI
1696–1757.
Architect, stage designer.

LARGE, CIRCULAR HALL WITH TWO TIERS OF COLUMNS.
Pen, bistre, brown wash.
494-590 mm.
Colls.: Piancastelli, Brandegee.
Janos Scholz, New York.

PALACE COURTYARD WITH SEVERAL ARCHWAYS.
Pen, bistre, brown wash.
277-405 mm.
This fine drawing, which came recently to the Metropolitan Museum, shows distinctive Bibiena elements and I would tentatively include it among the late works of Giuseppe Bibiena.
Metropolitan Museum of Art, New York.

TOWN SQUARE.
Sepia and water-colour.
The drawing was exhibited at the Museum of Modern Art, New York, 1943, Cat. no. 48, as by Giuseppe Bibiena; I am not too certain about this attribution because the penmanship is too fluid and nervous for him. Hyatt Mayor's suggestion of an early Juvara in the Bibiena style has definite merits.
Drottningholm, Theater Museum.

30 DESIGN FOR A LARGE HALL WITH A THRONE OR AN ALTAR IN THE CENTER; RIGHT PORTION.
Pen, bistre wash.
215-158 mm.
Coll.: E. Tinto.
A. M. Friend, Princeton, New Jersey.

31 HALL WITH STAIRCASE.
Pen, bistre, gray wash.
290-204 mm.
Colls.: Piancastelli, Brandegee.
A. M. Friend, Princeton, New Jersey.

32 DRAWING FOR A LARGE FUNERAL HALL, REMINISCENT OF THE COLOSSEUM IN ROME.
Pen, bistre, brown and gray wash.
409-549 mm.
Published: A. Hyatt Mayor: *The Bibiena Family*, pl. 39.
Colls.: Mayr, Fajt.
Janos Scholz, New York.

33 PALACE COURTYARD WITH COLUMNS.
Pen, bistre, gray wash.
226-320 mm.
Ricci: *I Bibiena*, reproduces a copy of this drawing as by Carlo Bibiena.
Colls.: Mayr, Fajt.
Janos Scholz, New York.

BIBIENA, ANTONIO GALLI
1700–1774.
Stage designer, architect.

34 ROYAL TENT.
Pen, bistre, brown wash.
227-365 mm.

Published: *Theatrical Designs*, vol. I, pl. 6. A. Hyatt Mayor: *The Bibiena Family*, pl. 42.

Colls.: Mayr, Fajt.

Janos Scholz, New York.

35 DESIGN FOR AN ORNATE ROOM.

Pen, bistre, brown wash.

263-435 mm.

Colls.: Piancastelli, Brandegee.

Walter C. Baker, New York.

36 LEFT PORTION OF A DESIGN FOR A TRI-UMPHAL ARCH.

Probably for a festivity in connection with a Habsburg victory over the Turks.

Pen, brown ink over black crayon.

415-291 mm.

On the back of the drawing is the inscription:

1721 Disegno del Gran Antonio Bibiena | Io Maria Ester Galli Bibiena | Bologna.

Published: *Theatrical Designs*, vol. I, pl. 5. A. Hyatt Mayor: *The Bibiena Family*, pl. 48.

Colls.: Mayr, Fajt.

Janos Scholz, New York.

See no. 24.

37 COURTYARD OF A PALACE.

Pen, brown ink over black crayon.

338-452 mm.

Colls.: Piancastelli, Brandegee.

Janos Scholz, New York.

38 INTERIOR OF A RECEPTION HALL, WITH A DOOR LEADING INTO A DINING ROOM.

Pen, bistre, gray wash.

Late in style, like a drawing for a façade

dated 1773, from the Piancastelli Collection.

Vienna Academy of Fine Arts.

BIBIENA, FRANCESCO

1659–1739.

Stage designer, architect.

39 PRISON COURTYARD.

Pen, bistre, gray wash.

247-368 mm.

Similar in conception and execution to the drawing in Vienna, reproduced by Gregor in *Monumenta Scenica*.

Janos Scholz, New York.

BIBIENA, CARLO

1728–1787.

Stage designer.

40 RIGHT PORTION OF A DESIGN FOR A GAL-LERY WITH SCULPTURES.

Pen, brown ink, gray wash.

208-251 mm.

This and the following 3 drawings belong to a rather large group of designs, which originally belonged to Piancastelli and are now scattered in various museums and private collections in America.

Colls.: Piancastelli, Brandegee.

Janos Scholz, New York.

41 HALL WITH COLONNADE LEADING INTO A PARK.

Pen, brown ink, gray wash.

197-291 mm.

Colls.: Piancastelli, Brandegee.

Ianos Scholz, New York.

CEPTION HALL.
en, brown ink, gray wash.
)8-292 mm.
olls.: Piancastelli, Brandegee.
nos Scholz, New York.

LACE COURTYARD WITH DOOR LEAD-
G INTO A PARK.
en, brown ink, gray wash.
4-293 mm.
olls.: Piancastelli, Brandegee.
nos Scholz, New York.

UVARA, FILIPPO
576–1736.
orn in Messina, the foremost architect
Piedmont, died in Madrid.

COUNTRY HOUSE OR MILL ON A RIVER.
tage set for the Cardinal Ottoboni,
ome.
en, bistre, brown wash over black
halk.
urin, Biblioteca Nazionale.

ARGE HALL AND PALACE COURTYARD.
ATRIO REGGIO.")
en, bistre, brown wash, over black
halk.
or the theatre in Turin.
urin, Biblioteca Nazionale.

TERIOR OF A CHURCH.
ated 1729.
en, bistre, brown wash over black
halk.
urin, Museo Civico.

ARGE HALL AND STAIRCASE; LEFT POR-
ON.

Pen, bistre, brown wash over black chalk.
284-371 mm.
On the verso: Sketches for side wings.
Colls.: Piancastelli, Brandegee.
Janos Scholz, New York.

GALLIARI, BERNARDINO
1707–1794.
First important member of this large family of stage decorators, who dominated Piedmont after the death of Juvara. Bernardino Galliari worked in Lombardy, Piedmont and Germany.

48 STAGE SET FOR AN OPERA, "CAIUS MARIUS."
Pen, india ink with red ink corrections.
284-415 mm.
Contemporary inscription: *Jugurtha usurpator del regno della Numidia e tiranno, Mario lo conduce in trionfo e poi lo fece morir di fame in prigione con due suoi figli.*
This and the following sets by Bernardino Galliari have been made for the theatre in Turin, about 1760.
Published: *Theatrical Designs,* vol. I, pl. 11.
Colls.: Mayr, Fajt.
Janos Scholz, New York.

49 SET FOR AN OPERA, "ALEXANDER THE GREAT."
Pen, bistre over red chalk.
283-418 mm.
Contemporary inscription: *Alessandro nel tempio del Giove Amone, . . . chiamato dal Sacerdote figlio di Giove.*

Published: *Theatrical Designs,* vol. I, pl. 10.
Colls.: Mayr, Fajt.
Janos Scholz, New York.

50 COLONNADE WITH CIRCULAR TEMPLE.
Pen and ink, water-colour.
237-329 mm.
Colls.: Mayr, Fajt.
A. M. Friend, Princeton, New Jersey.

51 THE ELYSIAN FIELDS
Pen, bistre, wash over lead pencil.
375-455 mm.
Published: *Theatrical Designs,* vol. I, pl. 14.
Colls.: Mayr, Fajt.
Janos Scholz, New York.

GALLIARI, FABRIZIO
1709–1790.
Stage designer, architect, worked in Lombardy, Piedmont and Vienna; brother of Bernardino.

52 LEFT PORTION OF A HALL, LEADING INTO A SQUARE WITH FOUNTAIN OF NEPTUNE.
Pen, bistre, gray wash over black crayon.
404-268 mm.
Colls.: Piancastelli, Brandegee.
Janos Scholz, New York.

53 COURTYARD OF A SMALL PALACE.
Pen, bistre, gray wash over black crayon.
290-397 mm.
Colls.: Piancastelli, Brandegee.
Janos Scholz, New York.

GALLIARI, GIOVANNI
1746–1818.
Stage designer, son of Fabrizio.

54 FUNERAL HALL. ("AULA SEPOLCRALE."
Pen, bistre, brown and gray washes.
220-301 mm.
Colls.: Mayr, Fajt.
Janos Scholz, New York.

GALLIARI, GASPARE
1760–1818.
Stage designer.

55 MILL ON A RIVER WITH A BRIDGE IN TH FOREGROUND.
Design for a night scene.
Pen, ink, gray washes, water-colour.
410-553 mm.
Signed, lower right corner.
Janos Scholz, New York.

56 INTERIOR OF A ROMAN BATH.
Pen, ink, gray washes, water-colour.
412-552 mm.
Signed, lower right corner.
Janos Scholz, New York.

57 OPEN HALL OF A GRANARY ON A RIVE WITH A MILL IN THE BACKGROUND.
Pen, ink, gray washes, water-colour.
417-552 mm.
Signed, lower right corner.
Janos Scholz, New York.

58 SEPULCHRAL HALL.
Pen, ink, gray washes, water-colour.
419-554 mm.
Signed, lower right corner.
Janos Scholz, New York.

MAZZI, VINCENZO

1748–1790.

Stage designer, born in Bologna, where he worked most of his life. He engraved his own designs and published them in 1776.

COURTYARD OF A FORTRESS.

Engraving.

From: *Capricci Teatrali,* 1776.

PRISON SET.

Engraving.

Signed: Vincenzo Mazzi Inven. Delt. et Inci.

From: *Capricci Teatrali,* 1776.

HARBOR SCENE WITH A BRIDGE AND BUILDINGS IN THE BACKGROUND.

Engraving.

Signed: Vincenzo Mazzi I.D. et Inc.

From: *Capricci Teatrali,* 1776.

A CANAL WITH BUILDINGS AND BRIDGES.

Engraving.

Signed: Vincenzius Mazzi I.D. et F.

From: *Capricci Teatrali,* 1776.

SERVANDONI, GIOVANNI NICOLO

1695–1766.

Painter, architect and stage designer, born in Florence, studied with Pannini, worked chiefly in Paris, 1760 in Vienna and died in Paris.

GROTTO WITH NEPTUNE AND SEA GODS; LEFT PORTION OF A GARDEN SET.

Pen, bistre.

240-195 mm.

This and the following two drawings come from a small sketchbook, which was found among the material left by Lorenzo Sacchetti after his death. Note the strong, personal character of Servandoni's penmanship, especially in no. 63, so very similar to the upper half of the well-authenticated drawing in Vienna, repr. *Monumenta Scenica,* II, pl. 16.

Colls.: Mayr, Fajt.

Janos Scholz, New York.

64 "CASTRUM DOLORIS." DRAWING FOR A LARGE FUNERAL MONUMENT.

Pen, bistre.

240-195 mm.

Colls.: Mayr, Fajt.

Janos Scholz, New York.

65 FORTIFIED TOWN.

Pen, bistre.

244-374 mm., on two sheets.

Colls.: Mayr, Fajt.

Published: *Theatrical Designs,* vol. I, pl. 7.

Janos Scholz, New York.

LAJOUE, JACQUES DE

1687–1761.

Landscape painter, architect, ornament designer, worked mainly in Paris.

66 TWO ARCHWAYS LEADING INTO A PARK.

Pen, india ink, gray wash, water-colour.

254-406 mm.

Signed, lower right margin.

Metropolitan Museum of Art, New York.

67 PARK SET, WITH COLONNADES.

Pen, india ink, gray wash, water-colour.

250-406 mm.

Signed, lower right corner.

Metropolitan Museum of Art, New York.

PIRANESI, GIOVANNI BATTISTA

1720–1778.

Architect, designer, engraver, born in Venice, worked mostly in Rome.

68 "FANTASIA ARCHITETTONICA."

Pen, brush, brown ink.

330-495 mm.

Published: *Theatrical Designs,* vol. I, pl. 9. Ch. de Tolnay: *History and Technique of Old Master Drawings,* fig. 142. H. Tietze: *European Master Drawings,* pl. 101.

This drawing, with its obvious reminiscences to the Fontana Trevi, is not decidedly a stage drawing, although it could have been made for a spectacular backdrop.

Janos Scholz, New York.

69 CIRCULAR HALL WITH THREE ARCHES.

Pen, brown ink, wash, over black chalk.

156-218 mm.

Contemporary inscription or possibly autograph signature in lower right corner.

One of the very scarce stage drawings by Piranesi; compare with the drawing at the British Museum, Interior of a church, reproduced Leporini: *Stilentwicklung,* pl. 271. This drawing belongs to a group which Piranesi himself mounted on heavy white paper and apparently signed himself; the whole group belonged once to Piancastelli and is now scattered all over the world. To my knowledge there are some in the Boston Museum, the Fogg, Cooper Union, Rijksmuseum in Amsterdam, a large group in London belonging to Mr. H. M. Calmann and the important lot in the Kunsthalle in Hamburg, which came there about 1915. Some time ago Fabio Mauroner in Venice told me about a large group of drawings by Piranesi, which he saw as a young man in Rome in a storeroom of the Borghese Palace; it is possible that our group of drawings is part of the Borghese lot, which Piancastelli, as curator of the Borghese Gallery, must have known.

Colls.: Piancastelli, Brandegee.

Henry Regnery, Hinsdale, Illinois.

COSTA, GIANFRANCESCO

1711-1773.

Venetian landscape painter, scenographer, and engraver.

70 A FARMYARD.

Pen, bistre, gray wash.

286-347 mm.

A companion piece to this drawing was in the Malmann Collection, Berlin (Lepke Auction, 1918, no. 29). This drawing was formerly attributed to Luca Carlevaris.

Colls.: Maison, Philip Hofer.

Janos Scholz, New York.

GALLIARI, FABRIZIO

1709-1790.

Stage designer, architect, worked in Lombardy, Piedmont and Vienna; brother of Bernardino.

71 PUBLIC SQUARE WITH FOUNTAIN, HARBOR IN THE BACKGROUND.

Pen, bistre wash.

324-463 mm.

Published: *Theatrical Designs,* vol. I pl. 22.

This drawing has recently been identified by Mercedes Viale-Ferraro as a set for the opera *Demetrio* (1761).

Colls.: Mayr, Fajt.

Janos Scholz, New York.

FOSSATI, DOMENICO

1743–1784.

Stage designer, decorator; worked in the Veneto, Friuli and Verona.

AQUEDUCT.

Pen, brown ink, wash.

248-353 mm.

This and the following drawings by Fossati, except no. 76, come from a sketchbook, which belonged to Sacchetti, passed through the hands of an obscure Viennese stage decorator, Janitz, whose name appears on some of the pages, and was acquired by Mayr. The book contains finished drawings, sketches and detail-studies on both sides of the sheets. Compare with the Fossati drawings in the *Theater-Sammlung* in Munich.

Colls.: Mayr, Fajt.

Janos Scholz, New York.

ARCHWAY.

Pen, brown ink, wash.

260-350 mm.

Colls.: Mayr, Fajt.

Dr. Walter Hugelshofer, Zurich.

GARDEN SET.

Pen, brown ink, wash.

248-353 mm.

Published: *Theatrical Designs*, vol. I, pl. 19.

Similar to the Munich drawing, reproduced by Tintelnot: *Barocktheater*, fig. 89.

Colls.: Mayr, Fajt.

Janos Scholz, New York.

75 "AULA SEPOLCRALE."

Pen, brown ink, wash.

248-353 mm.

Published: *Theatrical Designs*, vol. I, pl. 18.

Colls.: Mayr, Fajt.

Janos Scholz, New York.

76 HALL WITH STAIRCASE.

Pen, bistre.

330-470 mm.

Signed, lower right corner D. F.

Companion piece to this drawing is in the National Gallery of Victoria, Melbourne, Australia, which is fully signed by Fossati.

H. M. Calmann, London.

77 TRIUMPHAL ARCH ON A PUBLIC SQUARE.

Pen, brown ink, gray wash.

248-353 mm.

Published: *Theatrical Designs*, vol. I, pl. 16.

Colls.: Mayr, Fajt.

Janos Scholz, New York.

78 COURTYARD WITH ARCHWAY.

Pen, brown ink, gray wash over black crayon.

248-353 mm.

Colls.: Mayr, Fajt.

Janos Scholz, New York.

79 PALACE ON THE BANK OF A RIVER.

Pen, brown ink, gray wash over black crayon.

248-353 mm.

Colls.: Mayr, Fajt.

Janos Scholz, New York.

BELOTTO, BERNARDO
1720–1780.

Painter, engraver, worked in Venice, Germany, Vienna and Warsaw.

80 COURTYARD OF A PALACE.
Pen, bistre.
216-353 mm.

In 1759, during the Austro-Prussian war, Belotto left Dresden for Vienna, where he spent two extremely productive years; his activities as a "Vedutista" in the Austrian capital are well known; on the other hand one could only guess about his work as a stage designer. Up to now the only certain proof of his connection with the theatre is the large engraving of a performance in Vienna, *Le Turc Généreux,* and some stage designs, reproduced by Fritzsche in his monograph on the artist, as *Ideal-Veduten* on plates 25 to 31.

Among the drawings in the Mayr Collection I found a small group of stage sets with Italian inscriptions and measurements, some of which have been marked by an eighteenth-century hand in black chalk: CANALETI. After further study I was able to reconstruct quite an *oeuvre,* of which the above drawing is the most important item, having on the verso the fine Roman set, similar to the one reproduced by Fritzsche on pl. 30, and with all the inscriptions in Belotto's own hand. Our nos. 82 and 83 come from a loose-leaf sketchbook, containing stage designs of all kinds from the traditional prison scenes to typically German town sets; this book must have passed from Belotto to Lorenzo Sacchetti, who used the empty pages of it for his own designs.

Colls.: Mayr, Fajt.

Janos Scholz, New York.

See: H. A. Fritzsche: *Bernardo Belotto,* Burg, 1936.

81 PUBLIC SQUARE AND VARIOUS SKETCHES.
Pen, bistre.
Verso of the preceding drawing.
Janos Scholz, New York.

82 PUBLIC SQUARE AND CHURCH.
Page 39 of the sketchbook.
Pen, bistre.
198-238 mm.
Colls.: Mayr, Fajt.
Janos Scholz, New York.

83 ROMAN RUINS AND FARM BUILDINGS.
Page 58 of the sketchbook.
Pen, bistre.
198-238 mm.
Colls.: Mayr, Fajt.
Janos Scholz, New York.

SACCHETTI, LORENZO
1759–1829.

Stage designer, decorator, born in Padua, first training with Fossati; worked in Venice for the *Teatro San Giorgio Crisostomo,* left 1794 for Vienna; court painter and decorator of Emperor Francis II.

84 PALACE STAIRCASE.
Pen, bistre.
228-188 mm.
Published: *Theatrical Designs,* vol. II, pl. 4.
Colls.: Mayr, Fajt.
A. M. Friend, Princeton, New Jersey.

85 LARGE TENT.
Pen, ink, gray washes.
230-315 mm.
Published: *Theatrical Designs,* vol. II, pl. 3.

Colls.: *Mayr, Fajt.*

Janos Scholz, New York.

CLASSICAL TENT WITH FIGURES.

Signed, lower right corner.

Pen, bistre, gray wash and water-colour.

190-248 mm.

Published: *Theatrical Designs,* vol. II, pl. 1. Freedley-Reeves: *History of the Theatre,* fig. 224.

Colls.: *Mayr, Fajt.*

Janos Scholz, New York.

CONCERT HALL AND INTERIOR OF A TENT; ON ONE PAGE.

Pen, bistre, gray wash.

365-226 mm.

Published: *Theatrical Designs,* vol. II, pl. 9.

Colls.: *Mayr, Fajt.*

Janos Scholz, New York.

SKETCHES FOR VARIOUS HALL AND TENT SETS, WITH NOTES IN SACCHETTI'S HAND.

Verso of the preceding drawing.

Pen, bistre, gray wash.

LARGE, OPEN HALL WITH AN EQUESTRIAN MONUMENT; IN THE BACKGROUND AN ARCHWAY LEADING INTO A PUBLIC SQUARE.

Pen, bistre, gray wash.

330-463 mm.

Colls.: *Mayr, Fajt.*

Janos Scholz, New York.

COURTYARD OF A PALACE.

Set for an opera, "Caius Marius."

Pen, brown ink, wash.

190-229 mm.

Published: *Theatrical Designs,* vol. II, pl. 5.

On the verso note in Sacchetti's hand: *Cortili che corrispondono alle case di Fabio con giardini.*

Colls.: *Mayr, Fajt.*

Janos Scholz, New York.

CHIARUTTINI, FRANCESCO
1748–1796.

Stage designer, decorator and engraver, worked in Rome and in his native Friuli.

91 ANTIQUE TEMPLE.

Pen, india ink, gray wash on blue paper.

254-290 mm.

Identified and published by Dr. R. Berliner in the *Chronicle of the Cooper Union Museum,* vol. I, no. 8.

For the *Teatro Argentina,* Rome, 1780.

Colls.: *Piancastelli, Brandegee.*

Cooper Union Museum.

AUSTRIAN DESIGNER, about 1780

92 GARDEN SET WITH SMALL TEMPLE.

Pen, bistre, water-colour.

200-244 mm.

Published: *Theatrical Designs,* vol. I, pl. 24.

Probably by a late follower of Fischer von Erlach, like Schuetz or Hohenberg.

Colls.: *Mayr, Fajt.*

Janos Scholz, New York.

VINCENZO DAL RÈ. *Fountain, Courtyard, and Stairs.*

PLATZER, JOSEF
1751–1806.

Stage decorator, born in Prague, studied with his father and later, in 1774, at the Academy of Fine Arts in Vienna. The most outstanding native stage designer of Austria.

93 PALACE ON THE BANKS OF A RIVER.
Engraving by Norbert Bittner after Platzer.
Published Vienna, 1810.

94 DRAWING FOR THE ABOVE ENGRAVING.
Pen, bistre, gray wash, water-colour.
218-374 mm.
Colls.: Mayr, Fajt.
Janos Scholz, New York.

95 GARDEN SET WITH A PAVILION, SIMILAR TO THE ONE IN THE PARK AT LAXENBURG, NEAR VIENNA. (Through the kind information of Dr. Otto Benesch.)
Pen, ink, water-colour.
178-242 mm.
Published: *Theatrical Designs,* vol. II, pl. 17.
Colls.: Mayr, Fajt.
Maria Bittner, New York.

96 ARCHWAY IN A PALACE, LEADING TO A CANAL.
Pen, ink over pencil, gray wash, water-colour.
190-214 mm.
Colls.: Mayr, Fajt.
A. M. Friend, Princeton, New Jersey.

97 GARDEN SET FOR THE FOURTH ACT OF MOZART'S OPERA "THE MARRIAGE OF FIGARO."

Made for the Prague performanc 1786.
Pen, india ink over pencil.
430-158 mm.
Published: H. Graf: *The Opera,* pl. 4 P. Nettl: *Mozart and the Czechs,* in M sical Quarterly,* July 1941.
First sketches for the following, fin drawing.
Colls.: Mayr, Fajt.
A. M. Friend, Princeton, New Jersey.

98 FINAL VERSION FOR THE PRECEDING SE
Signed, lower right corner.
Pen, ink, gray washes.
340-438 mm.
Published: *Theatrical Designs,* vol. I pl. 12.
Colls.: Mayr, Fajt.
A. M. Friend, Princeton, New Jersey.

99 A BARGE UNDER THE ARCH OF A BRIDG
Pen, brown ink over pencil, gray was water-colour.
357-508 mm.
Colls.: Mayr, Fajt.
A. M. Friend, Princeton, New Jersey.

100 HARBOR SCENE WITH AQUEDUCT.
Pen, brown ink over pencil, gray was
348-508 mm.
Colls.: Mayr, Fajt.
A. M. Friend, Princeton, New Jersey.

SANQUIRICO, ALESSANDRO
1777–1849.

Stage designer, painter, worked for t Scala in his native city of Milan.

RDEN SET WITH CLASSICAL BUILDING
TED 1827.

uatint, coloured.

om: *Raccolta di Varie Decorazioni
·niche.*

ROTTO"; SET FOR THE BALLET
'ALUNNO DELLA GIUMENTA" BY SAL-
TORE VIGANO.

ted 1812.

uatint, coloured.

om: *Raccolta di Varie Decorazioni
·niche.*

TERIOR OF A PYRAMID; SET FOR THE
LLET "PSAMMI" BY SALVATORE VI-
NO.

n, ink, gray wash.

4-378 mm.

is is the original drawing for the aqua-
t published in the *Raccolta.*

l.: Giorgio Nicodemi, Milan.

ios Scholz, New York.

JAGLIO, GIULIO
54–1801.

ge designer, member of the large fam-
of artists who dominated their field in
nich for generations.

SON SET, WITH HALL OF A PALACE IN
E BACKGROUND.

n, ink, gray wash, light water-col-
r.

-168 mm.

blished: Freedley-Reeves: *History of
Theatre,* fig. 225.

ilar drawings are in the Theater-Mu-

seum in Munich. Through the kind information of Dr. Franz Rapp.

Janos Scholz, New York.

PIAN, ANTONIO DE
1784–1851.

Stage decorator, born in Venice, worked
most of his life in Vienna.

105 GREEK TEMPLE SETTING.

Pen, ink, water-colour on gray paper.
378-483 mm.

Published: *Theatrical Designs,* vol. III,
pl. 9.

Colls.: Mayr, Fajt.

Janos Scholz, New York.

106 ENTRANCE OF A GREEK FUNERAL TEM-
PLE.

Pen, ink, water-colour on gray paper.
369-483 mm.

Published: *Theatrical Designs,* vol. III,
pl. 8.

Colls.: Mayr, Fajt.

Janos Scholz, New York.

107 INTERIOR OF AN EGYPTIAN TEMPLE.

Set for "The Magic Flute" by Mozart.
Engraving by Norbert Bittner after de
Pian.

This and the following three sets are from
the book Norbert Bittner published in
Vienna, 1818.

108 EXTERIOR OF A TEMPLE, WITH PYRAMID.

Set for "The Magic Flute" by Mozart.

109 CEMETERY WITH AN EQUESTRIAN MON-
UMENT.

Set for "Don Giovanni" by Mozart.

110 ROMAN PUBLIC SQUARE.

Set for the opera "Titus" by Mozart.

NEEFE, HERMANN
1790–1854.

Stage designer and landscape painter, born in Bonn, Germany, and died in Vienna.

111 THE TEMPLE OF THE INCAS.

Set for the opera "Fernando Cortez" by Spontini; for a Vienna performance.

Brush drawing in gray ink.

240-298 mm.

Colls.: Mayr, Fajt.

Janos Scholz, New York.

GAIL, JOSEPH
Died 1830.

Austrian stage decorator.

112 DESIGN FOR A CLASSICAL CURTAIN.

Pen, india ink, gray washes.

190-270 mm.

Published: *Theatrical Designs,* vol. III, pl. 4.

Colls.: Mayr, Fajt.

Janos Scholz, New York.

BIEDERMANN, JOHANN
Worked around 1800.

Austrian stage designer.

113 SET FOR A GRAVEYARD.

Pen, india ink, water-colour.

194-314 mm.

Colls.: Mayr, Fajt.

Janos Scholz, New York.

BASOLI, ANTONIO
1774–1848.

Stage designer, worked mostly in Bologna.

114 "FUOCO." STAGE SET FOR A BURNING TOWN.

Pen, brown ink, wash.

208-304 mm.

Colls.: Piancastelli, Brandegee.

Cooper Union Museum.

115 PALACE OF MONTEZUMA.

Contemporary note: *Pensiero rappresentante l'America.*

A. Basoli inv. e fece.

Pen, brown ink, wash.

201-295 mm.

Colls.: Piancastelli, Brandegee.

Cooper Union Museum.

SCHINKEL, KARL FRIEDRICH
1781–1841.

Stage designer, architect and painter, the foremost classical-romantic decorator of Germany, famous for his superb sets for "The Magic Flute" by Mozart, for which opera he made twenty-six different versions.

116 "BURG RINGSTAEDTEN"; FOR THE LAST SCENE OF THE OPERA "UNDINE" BY LORTZING.

Coloured aquatint.

117 TEMPLE OF APOLLO; FOR THE OPERA "ALCESTE" BY GLUCK.

Coloured aquatint.

IEW OF JERUSALEM AND THE FORTRESS
F ZION; FOR THE OPERA "ATHALIA" BY
IEYERBEER.

loured aquatint.

ARGE GOTHIC HALL WITH A VIEW OF
HEIMS FOR SCHILLER'S "MAID OF OR-
EANS."

loured aquatint.

NSTITORIS

Vorked about 1830.

bscure stage decorator of Hungarian
rigin, who worked in Vienna and in
vestern Hungary; his interesting, exten-
ive notebooks, now in the Public Li-
rary, New York, contain immense ma-

terial about the theatres of Vienna of the
1820's.

120 GARDEN SET WITH FOUNTAINS; AFTER A
DESIGN BY ANTONIO DE PIAN.

Pen, ink, water-colour.

242-402 mm.

Published: *Theatrical Designs,* vol. III,
pl. 23.

Colls.: Mayr, Fajt.

Janos Scholz, New York.

121 DESIGN FOR A CURTAIN.

Pen, ink, water-colour.

263-360 mm.

Published: *Theatrical Designs,* vol. III,
pl. 19.

Colls.: Mayr, Fajt.

Janos Scholz, New York.

ACKNOWLEDGMENTS

We are grateful to the following institutions and persons for granting permission to
reproduce originals in their possession or lending us photos:

Drottningholm, Sweden, Theater Museum: no. 29.

Florence, Italy, Uffizi Gallery: nos. 1, 2, 4, 5.

Hinsdale, Ill., Mr. Henry Regnery: nos. 24, 69.

London, England, British Museum: no. 14.

London, England, Mr. H. M. Calmann: no. 76.

New York, N. Y., Mr. Walter C. Baker: no. 35.

New York, N. Y., Mrs. Maria Bittner: no. 95.

New York, N. Y., Museum for the Arts of Decoration of the Cooper Union: nos. 19,
20, 91, 114, 115.

New York, N. Y., The Metropolitan Museum of Art: nos. 3, 7, 8, 9, 10, 11, 12, 18, 25,
28, 66, 67, 101, 102.

Princeton, N. J., Mr. A. M. Friend: nos. 22, 30, 31, 50, 96, 97, 98, 99, 100.

Turin, Italy, Biblioteca Nazionale: nos. 44, 45 (Photos MMA).

Turin, Italy, Museo Civico: no. 46 (Photo MMA).

Vienna, Austria, Academy of Fine Arts: no. 38 (Photo MMA).

Zurich, Switzerland, Dr. Walter Hugelshofer: no. 73.

BIBLIOGRAPHY

This bibliography of stage design and architectural drawing includes some early collections of prints of stage sets, but no books on specific festivities.

ALBERTI, LEON BATTISTA:
De Re Aedificatoria.
Florence, 1485.

BARBARO, DANIELE:
La Pratica della Perspettiva.
Venice, 1569.

BASOLI, ANTONIO:
Raccolta di Prospettive serie, rustiche, e di Paesaggio.
Bologna, 1810.

BEAUMONT, CYRIL W.:
Five Centuries of Ballet Design.
London, 1939.

BEIJER, AGNE:
Slottsteatrarna på Drottningholm och Gripsholm.
Stockholm, 1937.

BIACH–SCHIFFMANN, F.:
Giovanni und Ludovico Burnacini. Theater und Feste am Wiener Hofe.
Vienna, 1931.

BIBIENA, FERDINANDO:
L'Architettura Civile.
Parma, 1711.

Die Bildbestaende der Theatersammlung Louis Schneider im Museum der Preussischen Staatstheater Berlin. Systematischer Katalog.
Herausgegeben von Rolf Badenhausen.
Berlin 1938. (Schriften der Gesellscha fuer Theatergeschichte)

Bilder fran Slottsteatern pa Drottningholm.
Malmö (1942).

BLOMFIELD, REGINALD:
Architectural Drawing and Draughtsmen.
London, 1912.

BUCHOTTE:
Les Règles du Dessein et du Lavis.
Paris, 1722.

Chronicle of the Museum for the Arts and De oration of the Cooper Union. Vol. I. N. August, 1941.

Denkmaeler des Theaters. Inszenierung, De oration, Kostuem des Theaters und der grosse Feste aller Zeiten nach Originalen der Th atersammlung der Nationalbibliothek, der A bertina und verwandter Sammlungen.
12 portfolios. Vienna 1924-1930.

EGGER, HERMANN:
Architectonische Handzeichnungen alter Mei ter.
Vienna, 1911.

FREEDLEY–REEVES:
History of the Theatre.
New York (1940).

GALLIARI, GASPARE:
Numero XXIV Invenzioni Teatrali.
Milan, 1803.

GAMBLE, WILLIAM BURT:
The Development of Scenic Art, a List of References in the New York Public Library.
New York, 1928.

GRAF, H.:
The Opera.
New York (1941).

GREGOR, J.:
Wiener Szenische Kunst. Die Theaterdekoration.
Vienna, 1924.

LANCASTER, H. C.:
Le Mémoire de Mahelot, Laurent et d'autres Décorateurs de l'Hôtel de Bourgogne et de la Comédie francaise.
Paris, 1920.

LINFERT, CARL:
Die Grundlagen der Architekturzeichnung, a Kunstwissenschaftliche Forschungen. 1931, vol. 1, pp. 133-246, 68 ills.

L'ORME, PHILIBERT DE:
Le premier Tome de l'Architecture.
Paris, 1567.

LOTZ, ARTHUR:
Das Feuerwerk.
Leipzig, 1940.

MARIANI, V.:
Storia della Scenografia Italiana.
Florence, 1930.

MAYOR, A. H.:
The Bibiena Family.
New York, 1945.

MAZZI, VINCENZO:
Caprici di Scene Teatrali.
(Bologna), 1776.

MOUREY, GABRIEL:
Le Livre des Fêtes Françaises.
Paris, 1930.

NETTL, P.:
Mozart and the Czechs.
Musical Quarterly, July, 1941.

NIESSEN, CARL:
Das Buehnenbild.
Bonn & Leipzig, 1924-1927.

OENSLAGER, DONALD:
Scenery then and now.
New York, 1936.

PLATZER:
Theater Dekorationen nach den Original Skitzen des Hof Theater Mahlers Joseph Platzer radiert und verlegt von Norbert Bittner.
Vienna, 1816.

POZZO, ANDREA:
Prospettiva de Pittori e Architetti. Parte Seconda.
Rome, 1700.

(RAPP, FR.):
Sueddeutsche Theaterdekorationen aus drei Jahrhunderten. (Jahresgabe fuer 1926 der Gesellschaft fuer das Sueddeutsche Theater).

RICCI, CORRADO:
La scenografia italiana.
Milan, 1930.

RICCI, CORRADO:
I Bibiena.
Milan, 1915.

SABBATTINI, NICOLA:
Pratica di Fabricar Scene e Machine ne' Teatri.
Ravenna, 1638 (photographic facsimile with German translation published in Weimar, 1926).

SANQUIRICO, ALESSANDRO:
Raccolta di varie Decorazioni sceniche.
Milan (1810-1828).

SCHINKEL, K. F.:
Dekorationen auf den beiden Kgl. Theatern in Berlin.
Berlin, 1819-1824.

SCHMITZ, HERMANN:
Baumeisterzeichnungen des 17. und 18. Jahrhunderts.
Berlin, 1937.

SERLIO, SEBASTIANO:
Il secondo Libro di Perspettiva.
Paris, 1545.

SIMONSON, LEE:
The Stage is Set.
New York, 1946.

TELLUCCINI, A.:
L'arte dell'architetto Filippo Juvara in Piemonte.
Turin, 1926.

Theatrical Designs from the Baroque through Neoclassicism. Introd. by G. FREEDLEY
3 vols.
New York, 1940.

TINTELNOT, H.:
Barocktheater und barocke Kunst.
Berlin, 1939.

VITRUVIUS:
The ten Books on Architecture, translated by Morris Hickey Morgan.
Cambridge, Mass., 1914.

WALLER, RICHARD:
A Catalogue of simple and mixt Colours, with a Specimen of each Colour prefixt to its proper Name.
London, Royal Society Transaction, 1686.

ZUCKER, P.:
Die Theater Dekoration des Barock.
Berlin, 1925.

ZUCKER, P.:
Die Theater Dekoration des Klassizissmus.
Berlin, 1925.

PLATES

1 BALDASSARE PERUZZI. *Street Scene.*

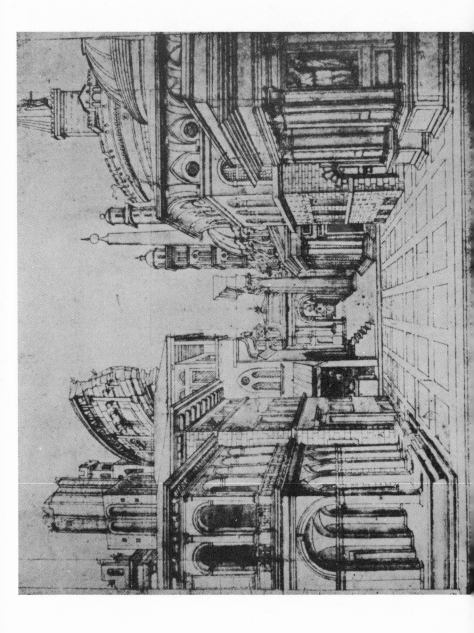

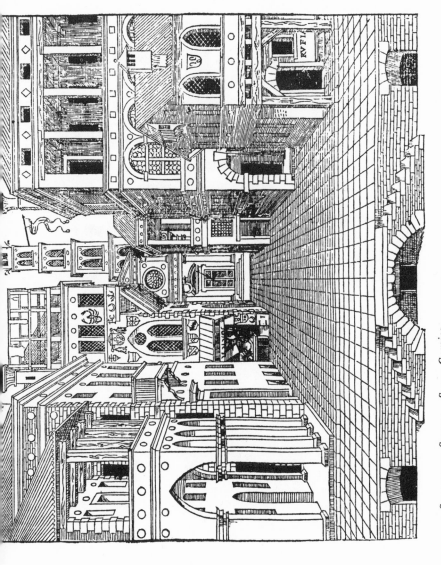

3 SEBASTIANO SERLIO. *Scena Comica.*

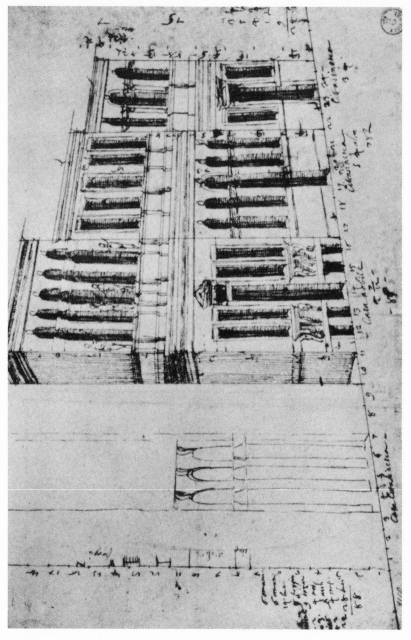

4 VINCENZO SCAMOZZI. *Street Scene.*

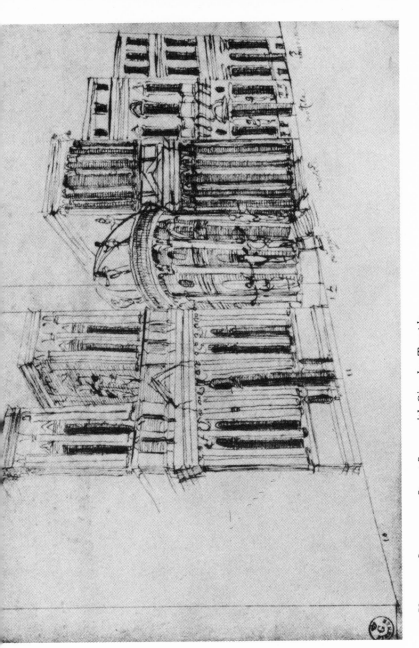

5 VINCENZO SCAMOZZI. *Street Scene with Circular Temple.*

6 SALLUSTIO PERUZZI. *Two Street Scenes.*

AVVISO DI MERCVRIO A BERECINTIA DEA DELLA TERRA, ET ALLE NINFE DE' CAMPI

7 GIULIO PARIGI. *Set for "Sbarco di Venere."*

8 GIULIO PARIGI. *"Intermedio Quinto di Vulcano"*

9 BERNARDO BUONTALENTI. *Street Scene.*

10. BERNARDO BUONTALENTI. *Naval Battle in the Courtyard of the Palazzo Pitti*

11 GIACOMO TORELLI. *Harbor Scene.*

48. Francesco Santurini. Scene VI for "Eadex Incoronato," by Riccoei.

13 STEFANO DELLA BELLA. *Council of the Knights of Malta.*

14. Giovanni F. B. Castiglione. *A Theatre Performance.*

15 LODOVICO BURNACINI. *The Temple of Vesta.*

16 LORENZO BURNACINI   Scipio's Palace

17 ANDREA POZZO.   *Drawing for a "Theatrum Sacrum."*

18 ANDREA POZZO. *"Theatrum Sacrum." An Engraving.*

19 MANTUAN ARTIST. *Courtyard of a Palace, with Proscenium.*

20 MIDDLE ITALY. *Palace Courtyard with Archway.*

21 MIDDLE ITALY. *Staircase and Hall with Columns.*

22 FERDINANDO BIBIENA. *Interior of a Bedroom.*

23 Ferdinando Bibiena. *Large Hall with Columns.*

24 Ferdinando Bibiena. *A Set for a Hall.*

25 FERDINANDO BIBIENA. *Palace Courtyard.*

29 GIUSEPPE BIBIENA. *Town Square.*

30 Giuseppe Bibiena. *Large Hall with Throne or Altar in Center.*

31 GIUSEPPE BIBIENA. *Hall with Staircase.*

33 GIUSEPPE BIBIENA.   *Palace Courtyard with Columns.*

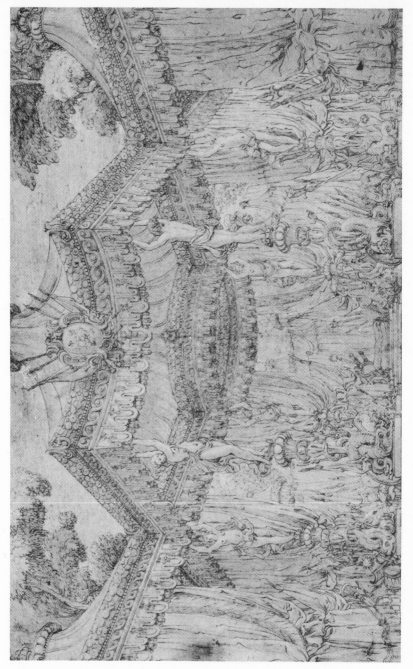

34 ANTONIO BIBIENA. *Royal Tent.*

35 ANTONIO BIBIENA. *Design for an Ornate Room.*

36 ANTONIO BIBIENA. *Design for a Triumphal Arch.*

37 ANTONIO BIBIENA. *Courtyard of a Palace.*

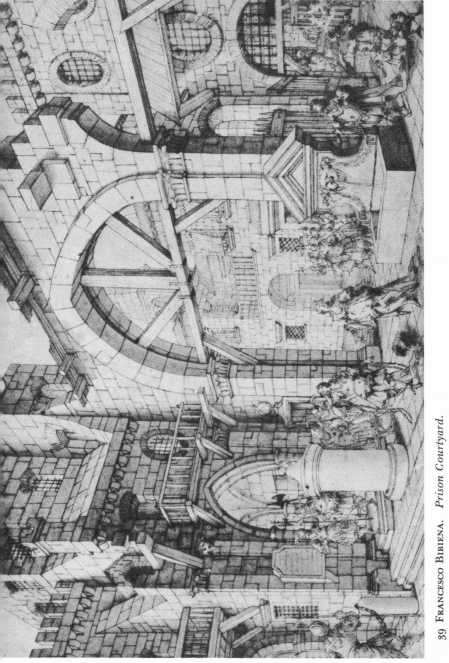

39 Francesco Bibiena. *Prison Courtyard.*

40 CARLO BIBIENA. *A Gallery with Sculptures.*

41 CARLO BIBIENA. *Hall with Colonnade Leading into a Park.*

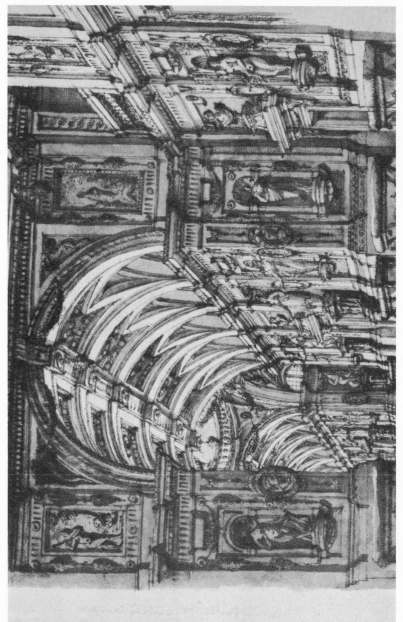

42 Carlo Bibiena. *Reception Hall.*

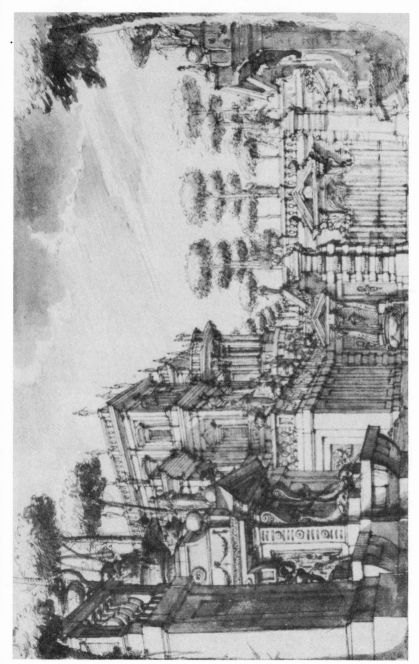

43 CARLO BIBIENA. *Palace Courtyard.*

44 FILIPPO JUVARA. *A Country House or Mill on a River.*

45 FILIPPO JUVARA. *Large Hall and Palace Courtyard.*

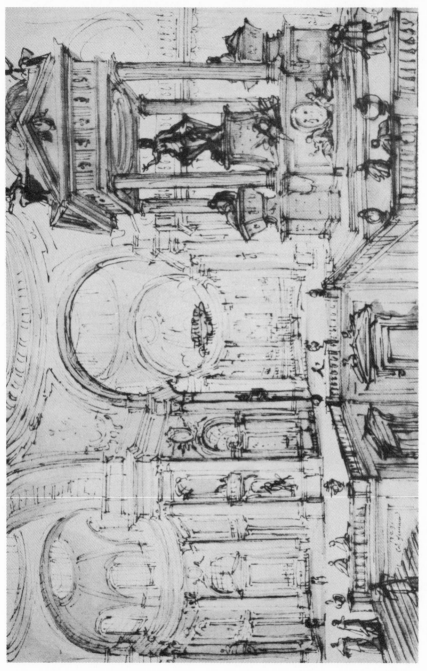

46 Filippo Juvara. *Interior of a Church.*

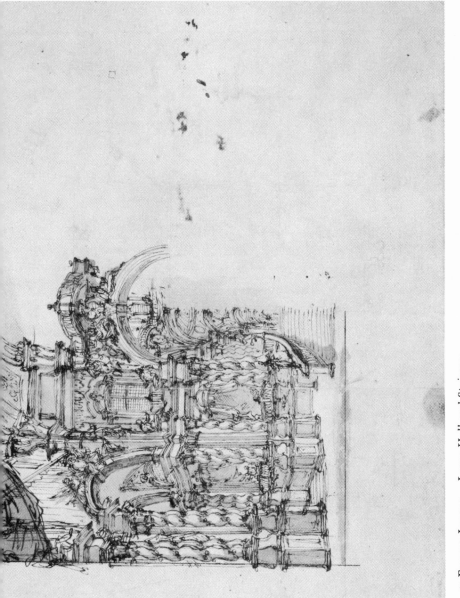

47 FILIPPO JUVARA. *Large Hall and Staircase.*

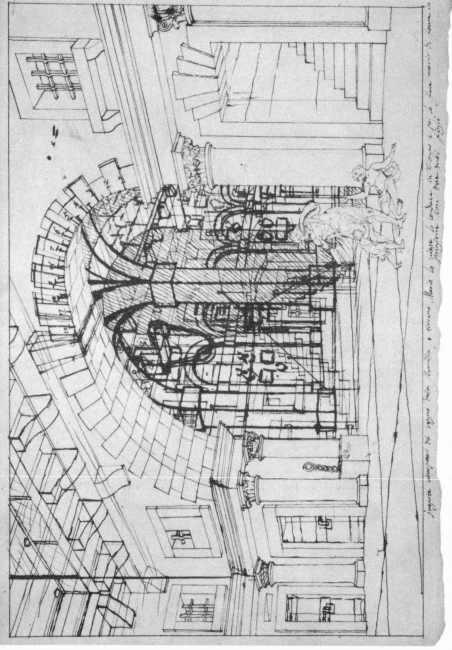

48. BERNARDINO GALLIARI. Stage Set for an Opera "Caius Marius"

49 BERNARDINO GALLIARI. *Set for an Opera, "Alexander the Great."*

50 BERNARDINO GALLIARI.   *Colonnade with Circular Temple.*

51 BERNARDINO GALLIARI. *The Elysian Fields.*

52 FABRIZIO GALLIARI. *Hall and Square with Fountain of Neptune.*

53 FABRIZIO GALLIARI.   *Courtyard of a Small Palace.*

54 GIOVANNI GALLIARI. *Funeral Hall.*

55 GASPARE GALLIARI. *Mill on a River.*

16. Gaspare Gasparri, *Interior of a Roman Bath*

57 GASPARE GALLIARI. *Open Hall of a Granary on a River.*

58 GASPARE GALLIARI. *Sepulchral Hall.*

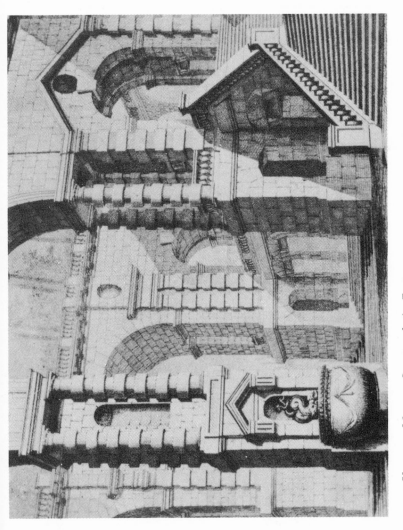

59 Vincenzo Mazzi. *Courtyard of a Fortress.*

60 Vincenzo Mazzi. *Prison Set.*

61 VINCENZO MAZZI. *Harbor Scene.*

62 VINCENZO MAZZI. *A Canal with Buildings and Bridges.*

63 GIOVANNI N. SERVANDONI. *Grotto with Neptune and Sea Gods.*

64 GIOVANNI N. SERVANDONI. *A Large Funeral Monument.*

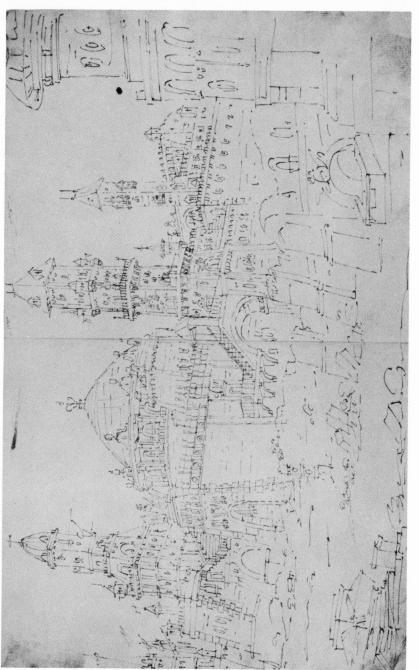

65 Giovanni N. Servandoni. *Fortified Town.*

66 Jacques de Lajoue. *Two Archways Leading into a Park.*

67 JACQUES DE LAJOUE. *Park Set, with Colonnades.*

68 GIOVANNI BATTISTA PIRANESI   *Architectural Fantasy*

69 GIOVANNI BATTISTA PIRANESI. *Circular Hall with Three Arches.*

71 FABRIZIO GALLIARI. *Public Square with Fountain.*

79 DOMENICO FOSSATI *Aqueduct*

73 Domenico Fossati. *Archway.*

74 DOMENICO FOSSATI. *Garden Set.*

75 Domenico Fossati. *Funeral Hall.*

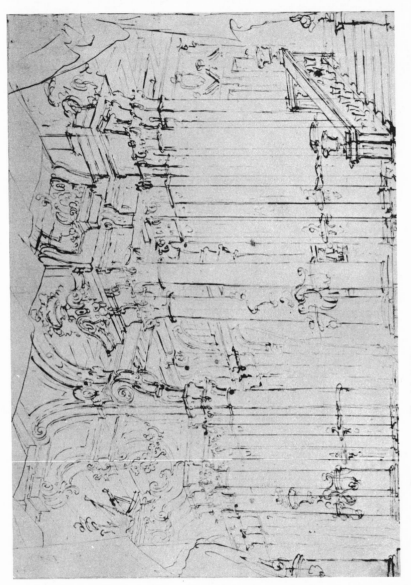

76 DOMENICO FOSSATI. *Hall with Staircase.*

77 DOMENICO FOSSATI. *Triumphal Arch on a Public Square.*

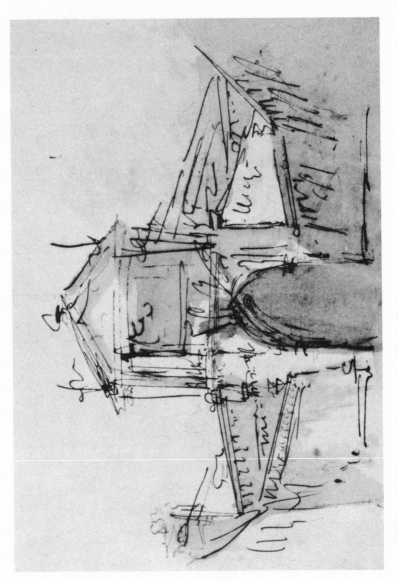

78 DOMENICO FOSSATI. *Courtyard with Archway.*

79 Domenico Fossati.   *Palace on the Bank of a River.*

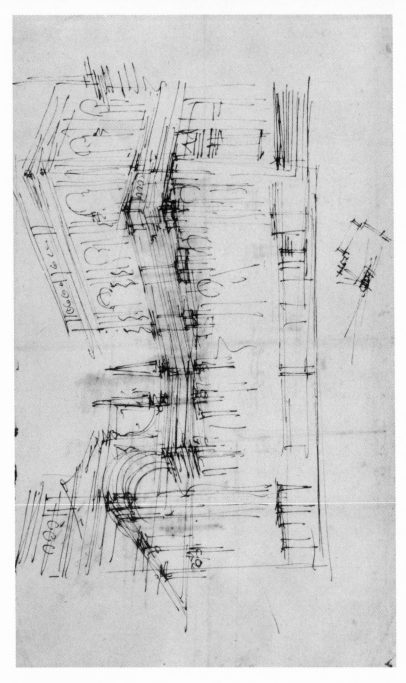

80 Bernardo Belotto. *Courtyard of a Palace.*

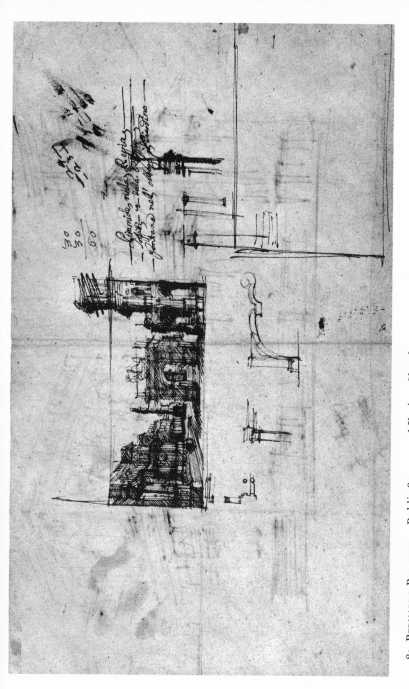

81 BERNARDO BELOTTO. *Public Square and Various Sketches.*

82 Bernardo Belotto. *Public Square and Church.*

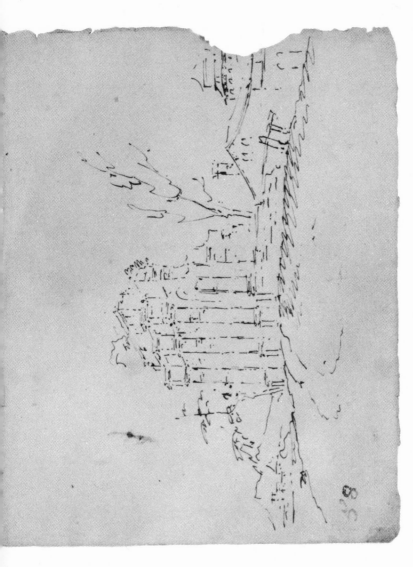

83 BERNARDO BELOTTO.   *Roman Ruins and Farm Buildings.*

84 LORENZO SACCHETTI. *Palace Staircase.*

85 LORENZO SACCHETTI. *Large Tent.*

86 LORENZO SACCHETTI. *Classical Tent with Figures.*

87 LORENZO SACCHETTI. *Concert Hall and Interior of a Tent.*

88 Lorenzo Sacchetti. *Sketches for Hall and Tent Sets.*

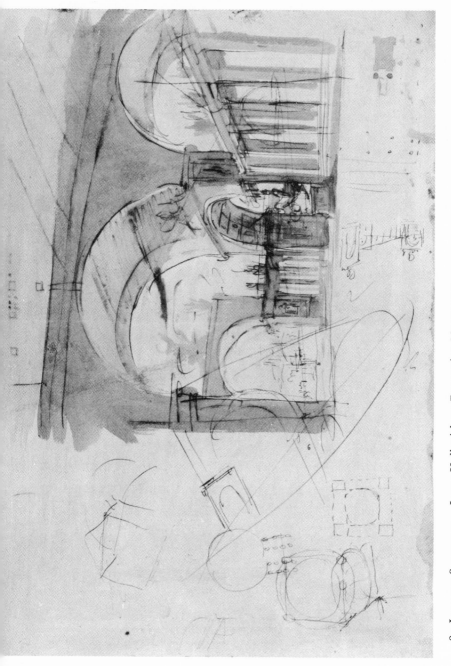

89 Lorenzo Sacchetti. *Large Hall with an Equestrian Monument.*

91 FRANCESCO CHIARUTTINI. *Antique Temple.*

93 JOSEF PLATZER. *Palace on the Banks of a River. An Engraving.*

94 JOSEF PLATZER. *Drawing for the Engraved Palace Scene of Illustration #93.*

95 JOSEF PLATZER.   *Garden Set with a Pavilion.*

96 JOSEF PLATZER.   *Archway in a Palace.*

97 JOSEF PLATZER. *First Sketches for the Garden Set in Fourth Act of Mozart's "The Marriage of Figaro."*

98 JOSEF PLATZER. *Final Version of the "Figaro" Garden Set.*

99 JOSEF PLATZER. *A Barge Under a Bridge.*

101 ALESSANDRO SANQUIRICO. Garden Set with Classical Building.

102 ALESSANDRO SANQUIRICO. *"Grotto" Set for a Ballet by Salvatore Vigano.*

103 ALESSANDRO SANQUIRICO. *Interior of a Pyramid; Set for the Ballet "Psammi" by Vigano.*

104 GIULIO QUAGLIO. *Prison Set, with Hall of a Palace in Background.*

105 ANTONIO DE PIAN. *Greek Temple Setting.*

07 ANTONIO DE PIAN. *Interior of an Egyptian Temple; Set for Mozart's "The Magic Flute."*

108 ANTONIO DE PIAN. *Exterior of an Egyptian Temple; Set for Mozart's "The Magic Flute."*

109 ANTONIO DE PIAN. *Cemetery with Equestrian Monument; Set for Mozart's "Don Giovanni."*

110 ANTONIO DE PIAN.   *Roman Public Square; Set for Mozart's Opera "Titus."*

111 HERMANN NEEFE.   *The Temple of the Incas.*

113 JOHANN BIEDERMANN. *Set for a Graveyard.*

114 ANTONIO BASOLI. *Stage Set for a Burning Town.*

115 Antonio Basoli. *Palace of Montezuma.*

116 K. F. SCHINKEL. *Last Scene of the Opera "Undine" by Lortzing.*

117 K. F. SCHINKEL. *Temple of Apollo; Set for Gluck's "Alceste."*

118 K. F. SCHINKEL. *View of Jerusalem; Set for Meyerbeer's Opera "Athalia."*

119 K. F. Schinkel. *Large Gothic Hall with View of Rheims; Set for Schiller's "Maid of Orleans."*

120 INSTITORIS. *Garden Set with Fountains.*

121 INSTITORIS. *Design for a Curtain.*